LA MOVIDA

TATIANA LUBOVISKI-ACOSTA

LA VIDA

NIGHTBOAT BOOKS

NEW YORK

ISBN: 978-1-64362-146-3

Interior and cover art by Tatiana Luboviski-Acosta
Design and typesetting by Kit Schluter
Typeset in Horley Old Style and Berthold Akzidenz Grotesk

Cataloging-in-publication data is available from the Library of Congress

Nightboat Books
New York
www.nightboat.org

CONTENTS

FOR THE LEO

When they wrest what we love most from us, the possibility of justice no longer exists. When the word justice loses meaning, all that remains for us is the defense of memory, of self-defense.

Mirtha Luz Pérez Robledo, tr. Scott Campbell

I want to be there, on the far side of sin /
I've been putting myself through hell, waiting for hell to begin.

Magazine, "Sweetheart Contract"

AGON

once, while on a coke binge,
and away from my mother,
my father drove his car
across the sand
and into the pacific ocean.
before doing that,
he had given away
all of his possessions,
and eaten
a steak dinner.

he survived.
and then,
he was able
to torture us
with his aristocratic ascetic drama
for years to come.
you can take a pisces
to water,
and all it will do
is challenge them
to cry more than the sky;
i say this with admiration.
how would it serve me
to make this up.
like my father,

i sometimes threaten
to succumb to wounds
and don the trappings
of desires
disguised as needs.
you may know them:
the sensible shoe;
the classical beauty;
the manicured hand
offered in neoliberal compromise.
i once told konrad
about how i successfully destroy
my attraction to strangers.
i imagine them standing above me,
as i lay prone
before them in their bed,
watching as they try
to get themselves
hard and or wet.
then i imagine
their sheets,
the hovering echo
of their mother,
the amount of humidity
in their bedroom,
if they put music on,
how their underwear
tucks in and around
their ass —

and usually,
around this time,
i've lost all
interest in them—
"that is so virgo of you,"
konrad said,
admiringly.
"that is 1,000 percent virgo."
virgo could be
my gender, or
it could be
my sexuality.
virgo in narrative lust;
virgo in high fantasy;
virgo in unhappy ending.
i don't know
what i like more:
the desire, or
the agonizing pleasure
of self-torture.
i like girls, but
girls
don't seem to like me;
In That Way, at least.
i love women
and
i love men,
just as i love
all of g–d's creatures;

but that doesn't mean
that i want to fuck them,
or be fucked by them.
hotly spayed virgin
in heat that i am,
i don't think that
i have a gender,
but i can now
certainly have an orgasm.
i orgasmed
on my way
to the slaughterhouse;
i orgasmed
on the
kill floor.
i wouldn't say
that the struggle
is between
masculine and feminine.
there's nothing
that i'm attached to,
i assure you.
i pluck the sinew,
and hold the cup
marked by my lipstick
up to the cloud's mouth.
i acquire the fear
that i don't hear
the affect,

because i have
the affect.
i would say
that the struggle
is between
decidedly unmasculine
and afeminine.
the struggle
is between
indecision and not caring.
like all good
poor people and aristocrats,
i know how to have a good time.
why i refuse to
is my own problem.
like all good
leftists of a certain region,
i have never read marx
or the bible.
i know the gossip
well enough
to kneel and resist.
for example,
or perhaps,
for instance,
i was content enough
to be a corpse eater
among the lotus eaters,
and then a lotus eater

among the petroleuses.
and now,
i'm a petroleuse
among the corpse eaters.

SAW YOU IN MY NIGHTMARES /
SEE YOU IN MY DREAMS

If you try to cross
a river wearing a veil
of concrete and glass,
how long will it be before
the bomb goes off? If you wan

der the fermented
fields of soap, blindfolded and
with a daisy in the
barrel of your rifle, how
long will it be until you're

aiming at yourself?
Tell me, how many hands did
you have to hold when
you leaned forward to unlock that
door? My friend, who died a thou

sand deaths. It takes a
true coward to resist re
sisting while dan
cing in the dark.

QUIVER WITH JOY

I was seventeen
when my father died, freeing
me to dive into
the earth. I ate the flesh and
I opened my legs and I
bled into the dawn.
Sleeping amongst
the pigs and their shit
was grander than any
homecoming could be.

IN RESPECT TO CANCER

I once wrote a poem
with a line about mothers
who demand respect
because they are mothers—
why, I couldn't tell you,
either about their demands,
or my intentions.
Now, I realize,
there are women
who are sure
that they are women.
I like the moon alright,
but I'm here, sucking clay,
and pressing the subtle breath
of the earth between my thighs
But only chastely so.
I swim in you,
there are no waves.
I'm not exactly giving forth,
but I am also not buying
what you're selling.
The tide went so far out,
the life exposed
lay upon me so expectantly,
gelatinous jewels

unsuspecting of your wrath.
I surprised myself by knowing
that it was time to run.

VAGABUNDA

Dear mamá,

This binary
is killing me.

HAPPINESS

Just because I did
it today, doesn't mean that
it doesn't need
to be done again and again
and again and again.

Was I my hands? Was
I my work? Was I your home?
In my time at the
bottom, in my time standing, wait
ing on the bouncy rot—

drowning while being
masculine in one language,
dying while being
feminine in another,
dead while neutral in this one—

Imagine if your
life was as long as a lake's.
You still won't live as
long as me. Cut me and
don't find the yellow flesh of

a plum.

THREE BISEXUAL TALES

"The Disappearing Man"

CAST:

PINK ZOTE SOAP as THE BOYFRIEND
ROSA VENUS SOAP as THE GIRLFRIEND
SILVER CHROME HAND-SHAPED RING HOLDER as GOD

The delicate hand
of God, resplendent in Her
demonstration of
likeness, reached down and grabbed the
Boyfriend, wasting away a

mong the waves. The Girl
friend watched from the shore, realiz
ing, with horror, that she could
see herself as she watched her
lover disappear. Later,

as she lay in what
was once their bed, next to
his indentation,
she found herself asking: was
it mercy? I saw him soft
ening in the tide,

I heard his cry for mercy.
His fragrance emerged
as I watched him choke on the
foam that he himself had bled.

She rose, and busied
herself with building an al
tar for him, laden
with her broken affection
and love. She wondered if an

yone else could ever
haunt her heart, unaware that
he had already
long disintegrated there,
too. It was mercy, she knew.

"The Bisexual"

CAST:

DIAMOND-SHAPED PRISM as THE WAKING LIFE BISEXUAL
PLASTIC DIAMOND ICE CUBE as THE INSECURE, DREAMING BISEXUAL
DESERT ROSE QUARTZ as THE LOVER
MIRROR as THE INSECURITIES
& FEATURING VAGINAL SCULPEY SCULPTURES
as THE BIPHOBIC UNCONSCIOUS

Their aura, their edge,
the cleavage of their
psyche lured her in.
She fell in love. They fell in
love. The two of them allowed

their love to expand
and be soaked by sweat, punk rock,
marigolds, and con
sommé. It oscillated
and throbbed like a sea of hair in

a mosh pit, nourish
ing them both with violence,
keeping an arms length
between the two of them. Yet
she felt safe, swaddled in a

16

rebozo of vel
vet and care. The feeling was
mutual, her lover
said through glasses of water
and limpias, their gaze a kiss
itself. When she was
alone or asleep, howe
ver, her Biphobic
Unconscious crept in.
Her mirror only showed her her

Insecurities
in aggressive detail. In
her nightmares, she was
swallowed by genitals, sur
rounded and mocked, as they tossed

her lover back and
forth, as if they were a ball.
Unable to in
tervene, she felt smaller and
smaller, suddenly plastic,

suddenly lighter,
her own facets dulling and
her insides freezing—
but then, she would wake up, come
to her senses, knowing her

desire wasn't so
brutal, so essentialist.
The morning sun would
remind her, as it cut through
her to say good morning with

a rainbow onto
the face of her lover, and
she would remember
that her love did not have
to be so complicated.

"A Wolf Woman in Paris"

CAST:

JACK O'LANTERN ELECTRICAL TEA LIGHT as THE WOLF WOMAN
SMALL PLASTIC LION FIGURINE as THE VISITOR / LUST
TURQUOISE TOOTHBRUSH as UNDYING AFFECTION
LARGE SPHERICAL PRISM as NEW MOON
& BUTTERFLY LINOCUT CUT-OUT, BUTTERFLY EARRING,
AND BUTTERFLY ENAMEL PIN as BLOODLUST

Before I was born,
and before you could remem
ber—so, once upon
a time, in…let's say…Paris,
AKA the Capital

of the white Imag
ination (you'll have to be
lieve me; and besides,
all the interiors look
the same to me in the Glo

bal North), a woman
was asleep in her apartment.
It so happened to
be the New Moon, and this sleep
ing woman had a condi

19

tion that caused a shift
in her way of being in
the world that was trig
gered by such celestial
events. So difficult, so
lonely, so predic
table was this cy
cle, that she had long aban
doned hope for any
kind of connection. Instead,
she maintained in her heart an

altar to an Un
dying Affection, and to
the kinds of sorrows
familiar to those who've
chiseled away the rose quartz

that flows through our veins.
As she slept, her memory
of a dollhouse not
even her own and a fire
she somehow set was placed

within a month-long
one-act play that consisted
of only her hand
coursing through a mane of some
kind, waiting for an unknown.

Still sleeping, her bo
dy underwent its transfor
mation, emerging
from below her belly while
also rising to the en

amel of her teeth,
alchemizing into Blood
lust. A Lion walked
into her room, over to
her, familiar and a

ffectionate. The Li
on lay down, against her rhyth
mically rising and
falling form, their heat expand
ing deep into her body,

deep into where her
dreams and sorrows lived and worked.
The transformation
unfolded itself. Her hand
reached for the—her—Lion's mane.

GÜEY

Galeano writes
that after Che's assassi
nation, novias es
queletos all over Ar
gentina emerged. My mom

says, you know Che's first
wife was an Acosta – a
matrilineal
one, at that. Never mind that
Hilda Gadea was Pe

ruvian, not from Tucu
mán; or that my mom was a
patrilineal
one; or that the Acostas
of my mother were anarchists.

This is the same wo
man who told my father that
naming their child Che
was the equivalent of
naming their kid Güey, or Dude.

Foo, ¿magínate?
Me being named Güey.

Like, after a use
less death, becoming the san
to noviequis of
anyone that ever looked

both ways before crossing Fig
ueroa to get to the
nail salon on
the other side, thinking sex
y thoughts against gang injunc

tions or gentrifi
cation; who knew the taste of

zucchini fries; who
ever lit a fire in the
middle of the street as a

distraction, kissing
the inside of their mask while
remembering the
soft bottom of the Glendale
Narrows against the tips of

their fingers. Yet on
ly you could say, oh yeah. Güey.
They once breathed into
my neck, sucked the Hot Cheeto
dust off my fingers, and called

their love for me the
terrain to which the ordinary
descend, and where their
heart was trapped, and then shotgunned
a kiss. That foo. Güey. Fuck them.

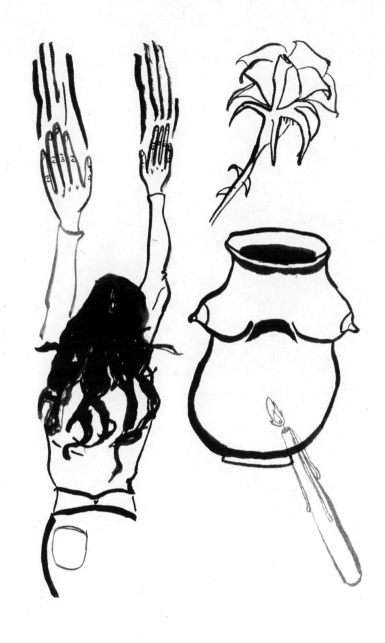

ICON B / W TOCAYO

Was she named
after the true image—

(telenovela star
turned
murdered friend)

or,

(boarding school lesbian
turned
revolutionary buried in the river)

or,

(ice queen
turned
headless virgin)

was the true image
named after her.

TATIANA LUBOVISKI-ACOSTA

I want the freedom
to make art about nothing
in particular.
Nothing is stopping me—
nothing, except for you.

¡Ándale, mucha
chita, vaya! Can you pro
nounce yourself in the
words they gave you? At
some point, we're all going to

have to face that a
lot of our ancestors were
just regular—not heal
ers or curanderas or
warriors—whatever we want

to claim—they were reg
ular people. Maybe they
believed maybe they
didn't maybe they spoke out
and organized against that

state. Maybe they're crin
ging and angry at us for
learning Nahuatl
—I know way way back mine
probably are—but closer,

they spoke with double
tongues. Actually, now they do,
too—low and deep as
if to be able to float
above your hearing. You know,

sometimes I like to
jump that fence, back and forth. When
my hair is parted
in the middle, I'm a boy;
when my hair is parted on

the side, I'm a girl.
On Fridays, we eat Filet

-o-Fish for lunch and
we light two candles at din
ner. If you can't already

tell, my entire last name is
a narrative of aban
donment—it could have
been worse. I could have been that

deep breath, that striking
lingual flirtation before

the objection.

SLAYER

I like the thought
of being denied
the new life
before I've even finished
the old life.
Hand over heart,
head over heels,
a season in purgatory,
a year in the dark,
within the circle
yet beyond the core.
House to house,
over doorways,
and at the head of the table—
light the candles,
lay down the salt—
I'll go ahead
and keep what's mine,
a glint of lead
heavy in its years of denial,
desperately wanting to melt.

AKTAION

Do you remember
that night so rich and pure in
its weight? I had come to
be fed by the cold, braiding
stream, then did something stupid
as I allowed myself
to be cradled—which is to say,
I fell in love
with them, the very person whose
presence allowed me to
be torn apart.
They cut through the trembling surface
of gem, with such ease in such a form,
their image scattering light
across their temporary self.
Later, as they transformed
into newborn eyelash, their westward body
turned me into something
sentenced to be pierced and eviscerated.
I should mention now,
that the joy of holding such
an ecstatic tension so disorienting
to my blood,
was well worth the punishment
for looking.

YOUNG GOD

You wonder
why I turn
away from you
in the night.

My lust
is a setting sun, my
hell is very lonely.

I was
murdered by my
desire. All
our friends looked

in all
the fountains
for my body;
and they never found me.

When god
was young, god
was everywhere.
Back then, the sky

made love
to everyone:

the rivers; the lakes;
and the oceans too.

In the beginning,
was the word;
then came the flesh.
And in the end,

all that was left
was the wound.
Young god trapped in amber.
I knew it in my body.

Their wrath
was verdant,
and tears of sap
smote their people.

Back here
in the same room,
my eyes follow you
from flower to blood

through the tear gas.
I lie across our bed,
still sexy,
but useless.

Look around you.
I have become a flood.
All things in my path
have found themselves

destroyed.
You took my hand.
I really only desire one thing,
my so-called love.

MEMORY OF WATER

There has got to be
a name for that condition
of destruction in
which an object becomes more
fragile the more it is admired.

It's the early violence
that I am glad to miss.
To imagine a string pulling the top
of my head up and in line
with my leg—a love

ly smile of abjection takes
the strain. A wretched
joke of community. A
ceremonial shard. A
cyclical cut. A

pose of tight thighs
bleeding forever.
I'd been neglected to have been told
of a snake below my belly
that communes with the moon

and the waves.
It sheds its skin,

it eats its tail.
It knows too much about me.

NO WAVE

The furnishings of
my swallowed house—broken bed,
bruised thigh, bleeding cer
vix—sit with me. Things
float into the air in protest.

Y me preguntan,
"What's your deal?"
My braid looks to
the curving future,
while my hem
refuses to answer.

SONG AGAINST THE WOUNDED HAND

The dancing water
replaced my tongue with a knife.
I watched you look past
me when you told me you loved
me. Behind the mirror were the

stars, and among the
waxing and waning head of
the disrespectful
daughter, they stood shining. As
the hours passed, they folded

into themselves, one
by one, until there was dark
ness. I stopped wear
ing the woven universe
when my face stopped being a map—

or rather, when the
map began to lead to a
ruin. In the town
of liars and poets, the
tumbleweeds having been re

placed by the rotting
silk garments in the colonial

style, I was torn
to pieces by the wild
dogs, yet stayed with you. My ribs

became your house, you
wove my hair to carry water,
and you used my tears
to adorn yourself. Clapstick.
Plastic bag surfing the waves.

Eternal fart o
ver the ocean. Acorn mush
cooking in asphalt
dimple. A dancing ruby
false in a paper cup. A

holy song sang by
the willow as it's scraped. Your
dress of cormorant
feathers glances green like the
ocean. But what good is the

new life? Our souls were found,
then saved by a stranger god,
whose children went a
head and murdered us any
way with green corn. Only say

the word! And I shall
be healed. My voice now carries
the lash of a law
that I do not respect. Bring
me the head of Junipero Serra

on a platter of
tar and gold, and your heart, roast
ed in the lap of
a chacmool. I declare war
on a war that I have inherited.

LLORONA

Trust me: This wail
is stronger than concrete, it's
louder than rust. It
is crueler than your lash and
your god and will brand you deep

er than any pox.
It will turn back the moon five-
hundred-and-twenty-
nine years, it will slit your throat,
it will sink your ships, killer.

The oranges, the o
lives, the grapes will rot and the
wildfires will rule, and
how I will rise, how my tears
will bleed and how my children

will emerge from mined
harbors. I am amused that
you expected me
to swallow the eventual
spiritual murder of my

children by your hand,
tie the rope myself and hand

it over to you.
Trust me, killer: this
wail will drown you, too.

IN THE ROUND

ladder, double sided, wooden
ak-47, wooden
machete, wooden
ak-47, actual
machete, actual
single stalk of sugar cane
splinter from single stalk of sugar cane, inside bottom lip
length of braid, approximately 529 years in length
single banana leaf
chandelier of red baby bananas
silhouette of single banana leaf and chandelier of red
    baby bananas against blinds at dawn
mask of bells
skirt of snakes
coffee sack blouse
blue tin of nivea
exactly 529 grains of amaranth
the word TECUILONTIANI in cochineal
a single line of dialogue:

FIJATE MI AMOR:
CONTIGO, SOY LIBRE

"AGON"

I suppose you could say
my sexuality is like
a sidelong glance
entwined arms clapping
(1, 2)—
pas de deux in the rund,
backs to the axis.

For I
have discovered my fetish,
and it is for the insurrection.

THE PROCESS

We didn't trust the
process during our struggle
for and defense of
memory. They respected
our guns, but not us. In

stead, we let the lakes
and the land speak for us, their
possible song co
mmandeering the waves through the
radio equipment hid

den in the plaster
bodies of virgins and saints,
reminding us of
a possible beauty be
yond the crimes against our flesh.

We refused to be
reorganized, so their cir
cular talk tried to
cut us down. Instead,
we sang our floating tongues back

in time, back to those
who came before, whose resist

ance and survival
made us possible. Bellies
of virgins and saints echoed

with static. It is
n't violence, the vol
cano interrupt
ed, to turn sugarcane in
to a weapon. It's on

ly self-defense, an
act of undying love. Let's
go ahead! Disor
ganize ourselves towards that
possible beauty, we said.

MY FRIENDS, THE LEFTISTS

Having found yourself
escalated by yourself—

All the girls lied about you.
It was springtime there, and
they were busy, all bleeding
from taut nuptial braids and full
embroideries, in the depths
of patriarchy upheld
by matriarchs, in the

mania of performative vir
ginity, deciding which a
mong them would be the sacrifice.
In a circle they stood, and I
rode away from them, towards the
fire. That unholy moon of spin
sters and widows, pink with failed
love, swallowed the sky, finite and

eternal.

Having found herself
escalated by herself—

I don't care that the rapist head of
state missed the time of miniskirts. To
know you is to know true love: and to
know true love is to take the streets. She
is our friend, and she is fucking cra
zy! We grabbed at the carcass, shredding
and discarding its flesh. Singing the
same songs, the same themes, in polypho
ny, voices knives against the throats of

unloving lovers. Be absent from this
new birth! Refuse this new language! Make love
in this hell of hells! I could fall in love
with you, I said to this manifesto
of that tendency treasured by the lo
sers of the world (Funny running into
you here I've been in nightmares from here to
Vancouver to Tijuana to LA
and back again and I've never seen such
a pretty little idea such as

your bad self). I flirt with twelve-tone terror with the aggression of a doomed maiden, and we keep ev erything between the heart and lungs, guts enrap tured, throats aching with joyful mystery—I would be lying if I said that it wasn't beauti
ful and that it didn't hurt, she screams, still bleeding, with tears streaming down her face; but not a hair out of place, and her lipstick matching her nails, as the state-owned, for-profit plasma center burns to the ground behind her when the revolution comes to town.

Having found myself
escalated by myself—

How do I clean your grave if I can't find it, if you
yourself don't even know where you are? Is the cycle
even complete? I subsist only on marigolds as
I make my way through the ash and lye, under velvet ab
sence of moon. How do I want to remember you, my friend
of dancing hair and obsidian tongue, left-handed in fighting?
By your name that adorns the walls, simultaneous
ly a blessing and an indictment? By your gestures
of violent beauty, by the throbbing lunar glow
of your knuckles? Or by your words to caress and be caressed
by? No. I want to remember you by your laugh.

Your laugh that is the flaming rag in the glass bottle.
Your laugh that is the window yelling in high bell chime.
Your laugh that is the explosion taking a deep breath.
—Fearless and nocturnal and feral like evening prim
rose, it could even make the cervix reject sorrow.
—And of course you were armed, we were all armed in those days,
when we kept our razors in our hair our weapons in
the sofa and our feelings to ourselves. Those were the
days. Art Laboe on the radio, slow jam de
dications to our less fortunate friends on the in
side, pouring ones out and vowing to never smoke weed

again until the prisons burned to the ground and we
could all get high together in the incendia
ry shadow of state failure and liberation—those
were the days. We were in hell then, but hallucina
ting paradise. We are in hell now, kettled in a
parking lot, six feet apart and affection is hi
story. I never could have imagined love in this
landscape. In public, we deliberately confuse
forgetting for forgiveness, and we dig and plant our
solidarity gardens in mass graves. Peace is a
lie that we've welcomed into our mouths, but hide

under our tongues, hoping we can spit out before it
absorbs into our collective bloodstream. Oh, my
friend, since you've left, how we now riot in despair and
how, instead of suffocating, I want to run in
to the house on fire, I want to be crushed, I want
to be killed by what I know isn't mine but that I
built, naked and raw. I want to hide myself like I
hide my rage, I want to disappear like a breath bleed
ing into the night — Instead, my friend, I hold your
braid between my teeth when the revolution comes
back to town. I look over my shoulder. I look be

tween my legs. I remember. They forget.

AMARANTH

Alive out of spite,
a general strike, a knife
to upper lip, a
bright laughing clit, and raven
ous walls all throb for the means

of production. Teeth
of happiness catch the joy,
and bite the touch. Is
it the radical in me
that wants that communal suc

cor and to be e
viscerated by re
fracted adora
tion. I invite the rebellion
into my sickbed while my

love lies bleeding on
the interrogation room
floor.

LOVE POEM

I, / an intellectual / once loved someone pure of heart / who let their car get towed away. // The vein that connects / my heart to my mouth / is a ribbon tied around a bomb. // I was joking when I said / that I knew how to read. // My vote was cast / for kissing by the light / of a cop car on fire. // My mother tells me that / a garden is a prison. // She was beautiful, with a face / like a melting candle; / and I'm sure well loved, / and well documented. // I know my father had nightmares / of limbs of soap / hidden among tall grasses. // There is carnage in this empty lot. // I cemented my banks / against the burning plain, / and drank the wine / that flowed from the wounded hand. // All day / and all night / in complicated love. // I loved someone / who loved the spirit in the sky, / so I tried / to fall in love with the sky.

PUSSY OF DREAMS

I am looking for a fight.
Look at me
in the landscape
from a nightmare of
romance.
—so let's sing against
our very own love languages
and transform ourselves into a fire
started counter-punctually.
The net is pierced,
the tongue is drowning.
It all remains the same
around the eye.
Silver mire
suffocates the illusion
while the image decays.
Subdue the struggle
with your thighs,
and pull the strands
from between the folds.

MEN WHO CANNOT LOVE

In the virginal springs
of my false childhood,
I consecrated myself
to the holiness of not
giving a fuck.
I have, of course,
taken that plunge
into the diamond sea
of men who cannot love;
you know how I love
to gorge myself
on the future ruins
of intimacy.
There's a weapon I wish
I could wield
when I feel the vomit of your gaze
hit the side of my face.
I want an education
in remembering
and I want an education
in forgetting.
I fast until the basket is done,
throw my maidenhead into the trash,
and relish the solidarity
of absolute feminine horror.

THE SLEEPLESS WATER

All I needed then was
a certain intoxication,
one procured
by mundane or
divine love.
Tell me how
our veins braided themselves,
dragging us into
a sure and sudden death
in the sleepless water.
I wanted you
to unfold me
beneath the surface of the river
that flows on the border of hell
and the bedroom-eyed face
of the moon goddess
with bells on her cheeks.
The tears of a false love
went ahead and rusted
my silver hands
as you sucked out my gender,
entwined with the marrow.

NUNCA MUERO

I am unsure of
when loving you became such
an act of war. The
barren woman, the lulla
by, and the unruly daugh
ter formed a coa
lition of evening and mor
ning star holding hands.
You can't see me if you don't
recognize my violence.
Voice cuts the skin, the
words come along, and I will
be alone. Can you
remember when your name was
my language, your embrace was
my country? This was
before the pressure of life
lived under a name
like a bitter sea while
standing on the hollow of
the moon's belly, be
fore becoming everything
I had resisted.
To live in what I thought was
love, I wore this performance
like a glove.

REMEDY

One day after you and
me, a jaguar came in
to my house. Not know
ing why, and my resistance,
like myself, being weak, I

gave myself over
to them. They dragged me outside
and into fists and
joy against discontent. Wan
dering hand in hand with a

certain void, I looked
for you on the barricade.
I looked for you through
the broken window. I looked
for you in the milk being

poured into my eyes.
I would be lying if I
said I knew a better
way to deal with a broken
heart than a riot. There is

nothing like it to
mimic falling in love. Listen.

I know it was you
with my blood lucent on your
smirk. And like I had told you

that very last moment,
I still believe that one day,
you and me will find
ourselves together in the
streets again

HISTORIA DE UN AMOR

Let me tell you a
story, disguised as a poem.
I once helped look for
myself, and I once pretend
ed that I did not exist.

Cariño. Queri
do. Compañero. Cari
ño. Why would I make
this up? You live in the aftermath,
where the river meets the sea.

In the living rooms
of others, we're visitors
In the purgator
y of subcutaneous
conflict, all desiring our own

disappearance. If
they come for me in the night,
know that here, in this
bag, is the love of my life;
know that if I survive, I

plan to mock myself.
I am thirty now, a short

life lived and entrenched
in nonsense. There is nothing
that I want more than to for

get this stupid war,
to remember instead the
sodium veil at
its thickest, those titties that
I sucked into the Oakland night.

¡Ay! Can you believe
that I have never felt love,
never felt the grace
or the consensus or the
eroticism of fight

ing for, as opposed
to against?

CERCA DE TI

Far from where I want
myself, where the air is hea
vy with the shit of
the doomed and the lilting gold
of drought, her voice emerges

and cuts right through me,
singing and slaughtering the
words that have lived un
der my tongue, that sharp language
only found at the corners

of your eyes. Tangled,
tight, dry with blood and defeat,
my cunt lays down its
arms at the sight of your ear
against the lips of anoth

er. My gender watch
es with the heavily-lined black
eyes of a child sing
er, under a crown of puffy
dark hair. A song emerges

somehow, from the pain
ful pastel bows, lace, and ruff

les of her body;
yet hides behind the me
tal screen door, veiled by a mesh

of domestic bore
dom, wet trapo under foot.
The dip of the mel
ody drags me into the
dry lakebed of your dreams, count

ing my tears with the
tips of its acrylics. A
bove: a palm tree ex
plodes, melting a plastic rose
abandoned before below.

You: unaware, bathed
by the spectrum blurring, caught
in indigo and
Spanglish. By the bridge, mira,
look—you've already forgotten.

REVISION OF LOVE

Hot vespertine pan
ic and ineffectual
allure hold hands and
break glass together in love.

Bootleg war and bootleg peace.
Love is now hell. Fictional
pussy versus a
ssigned cop at birth versus scorched
earth policy. Make yourself

a late arrival with a
vengeance. Remember what I
once said, I would accept
nothing if that was what you
could give me. Fuck that. I want

the plumage. Back then,
I had a revisionist
history of love;
and now I live against all
that was taught me, against all

that you told me.

LEAVING IT UP TO YOU

Fucking altars into existence
blindfolded and gagged
on the boulevard of friends
I'd been meditating
among capital's singing bowls
their skirts in hand
as they turned
thru this mausoleum of future trash
pressing the ashes of the masters
into diamonds and soap
who is she
who are they
who is them
it's part of the process
ask for permission
to be hunted
and caught for food
your skin keeps us warm
your fat keeps us shiny
your flesh keeps us from killing each other
pure beauty
perfect love
only a fool
can break my heart
only I
can break my heart

I am a fool
and I broke my heart
the destroyer
of my sensual world
born a cloud breathed by a bitter sea
I fight the hexagon
I vomit the snake
that's holding the rose
years pass
opportunities fade
there goes I
jutting my jaw into the thigh gap
leading my decaying good looks
into the typing pool.

AÑO DESNUDO

It's funny how the
lack of an accent makes it
an asshole. I was
once a teenaged performance
artist, before I was an

adult one; if you
look me up, you'll see my tit
ties for free. A pair
of eyes and a thick curtain.
When you met me, I was not

in the mood for love.
Then I found myself choking
on fat and blood, melt
ed and feathered, carrying
a bell. Who else do you know

that was radica
lized by jealousy? I want
ed to gaze upon
the lips of sleepers, to spend
the full folding fan of night

together. I want
ed us to hover, be ac

tivated into
a blessed state. I wanted
us to tumble into a

landscape poisoned by
our masculinity. The
buildings empty; the
gardens growing in perpe
tual ardency; the ani

mals fucking, nause
ated by glowing, toxic lust.
Alienation
of affection is what caused
the official flower to

rot on my mantle,
and it decided to take
its vengeance on my
fantasies (I am sorry,
eternity, for making

you my enemy).
What did I expect? Mercur
y went direct the
day after I was born, and
reality was on a

smoking break, so the
simulation looped on back.
Don't you know, you're my
partner in misery. Just
don't look to me for the lyr

ic, and don't try to
look for me, either. Baby
baby oh baby.
You don't love enough for me.

LA MOVIDA

Here at the disco
rancho, we all get our own
white horse. The revo
lution survived like a seed
in a concrete block, it

lived under my skin
and it lived deep in your ass.
All of the love songs,
all of the B sides, they were
just organizing in plain

sight. Come here and sit
with me, put your head in my
lap, let me fill it
with confusing sex and sex
y confusion and go a

head and take a gaze
into this crystal ball. This
love isn't ready!
Let me phone a friend, let me
exchange a glance, and oh! how

I want to swallow
those petals that fall out of

your mouth. Come here and
lay with me, put your head be
tween my thighs, let me fill it

with historical
lust and lusty history
and go ahead and
take a gaze into this crys
tal ball. Let's be friends fore

ver. I want you to scold me,
I want you to question me,
and oh! tell me the
time of your birth, tell me where
you were born. That Cancer rising,

Aquarius moon
that rose out of bells and yell
ing and I share the
same sun and Venus—doing
the natal chart of a call

to arms and doing the
natal chart of a dicta
torship and doing
the natal chart of someone
you feel has the potential

of becoming a
comrade and then a synas
tric chart with yours—but
isn't it funny how one
can be the inverse of the

other? Ask me later
about how I live part-time,
dragging a new moon
into a studio apart
ment a couple blocks from here

and then gushing into
oblivion—forgetting
the excavation
of space necessary to
make that love undying, that

life anew, that world
we so desire, that truth
we already live
as true—but part-time, I swim
in the low tide of that con

jured surging flood, beck
oned by the paw of the eighth
studio apart
ment's tenant, someone I wish
had bad politics or at

least—the very least—thought I
was ugly. Part-time,
I'm a Scorpio, and a
pathetic one at
that. Afterwards, I pick up

the corpse of my heart and dis
card that sex and death
caul—that's my lingerie—
and then I roll that
new moon down Mission and back

into my part-time
insistence upon
existence as re
sistance as existence in
my rent-controlled apartment

—here, let me give you the add
ress, do you have time
in your busy schedule to
join the kill list working group?

When we get to
the inevitable cir
cular firing squad,
please braid my hair before the
blade brushes the nape of my

neck—but right now, let's
just submerge ourselves into
the bass and suck each
other's lipstick off and go
ahead and sweat on me, I'll

bring those books I told
you about over to your
job at the end of
your shift, we can talk about
them on the dance floor, OK?

ACKNOWLEDGMENTS

This book could not have been written without the emotional, financial, and temporal support of so many people.

Tlazocamati to my family. To my mother, whose chaos and dancing star of a heart I honor.

A tender thank you to Kimberlynn Acevedo, Josiah Luis Alderete, Elizabeth Ardent, Claudia Avila-Gibbs, Dicky Bahto, Ari Banias, Michael Beltrán, Amy Berkowitz, Olive Blackburn, Kyle Casey Chu, the comrades at CCSF Collective, Chris Cuadrado, Riley Davis, Steve Dickison, Angel Dominguez, Taylor Doran, Adele Failes-Carpenter, Margit Galanter, Jasmine Gibson, Raquel Gutierrez, Liz Harris, Nalani Hernandez-Melo, Tyler Holmes, Elaine Kahn, Hannah Kezema, Natalia Kresich, Justin Lawrence, Lauren Levin, Zack Lewis, Krizta Marquez, Farid Matuk, Michael McConnell, Greer McGettrick, Linda Oleszkiewicz-Gonzalez, Carla Orendorff, Steve Orth, Mara Poliak, Naomi Quiñones, Xarí Rivera, Raquel Salas Rivera, Brianna Skellie, Lena Soboleva, Nickie Tilsner, Shabina Toorawa, Brianna Torres, Matt Weathers, Anna Rosa Velazquez, Lukaza Verissimo-Branfman, Vickie Vertíz, and, Daisy Zamora.

Thank you to Lindsey Boldt, my editor, for taking a chance on what was then a DIY comic on being a bisexual insurrectionist and a few loose papers; and to the rest of the Nightboat Books crew.

I am eternally grateful to Konrad Steiner, for his unconditional love and partnership, for telling me that if I ever quit making art, he would stop talking to me.

And of course, to The Leo, whose privacy I am maintaining out of respect. Thank you for the correspondence, whether via mixtape or written word—still the perfect way to seduce someone whose Venus is in Virgo.

TATIANA LUBOVISKI-ACOSTA is a queer anarchist Nicaragüense American artist of Indigenous (Nawat, Lenca, and Chorotega) and Jewish descent. They were raised in Los Angeles, California, and grew up traveling and living across the western United States and Mexico with their mother, a cultural anthropologist. Tatiana's first book, *The Easy Body*, was published by Timeless, Infinite Light in 2017. They live in a rent-controlled apartment in the Mission District of San Francisco.

NIGHTBOAT BOOKS

Nightboat Books, a nonprofit organization, seeks to develop audiences for writers whose work resists convention and transcends boundaries. We publish books rich with poignancy, intelligence, and risk. Please visit nightboat.org to learn about our titles and how you can support our future publications.

The following individuals have supported the publication of this book. We thank them for their generosity and commitment to the mission of Nightboat Books:

Anonymous (4)
Abraham Avnisan
Jean C. Ballantyne
The Robert C. Brooks Revocable Trust
Amanda Greenberger
Rachel Lithgow
Anne Marie Macari
Elizabeth Madans
Elizabeth Motika
Thomas Shardlow
Benjamin Taylor
Jerrie Whitfield & Richard Motika

In addition, this book has been made possible, in part, by grants from the New York City Department of Cultural Affairs in partnership with the City Council, the New York State Council on the Arts Literature Program, and the Topanga Fund.